ALL THE THINGS I NEVER SAID

All the Things I Never Said

Natalya Muncuff

All The Things I Never Said

Cover Design by T.E. Black of T.E. Black Designs
www.teblackdesigns.com

Editing - Little Pear Editing
www.littlepearediting.com

DEDICATION

To you, for loving me when I couldn't love myself.

You know who you are.

CONTENT

ON MY SLEEVE

I've always been too distant.
Too cold.
Too practical.

Not allowing myself
to feel anything.
To appreciate anything or anyone.

To love fully.
To give everything.
To make magic.

I've never
taken enough chances.
Tempted fate,
felt the adrenaline coursing through my veins as I did
something reckless.

Never said I loved you to the one who deserved it,
never bared my soul except among the pages of well-worn
journals.

I've always been too much
yet not enough.

But now, I choose to give all of myself.

Not in hopes of acceptance
or in search of someone I let slip away.

But so I can live my truth and tell my stories.
Unlock my soul,
and wear my heart on my sleeve, for all to see
and know that it's okay
if you want to do the same.

PERMISSION

Everything we need, we already have.
We just need to give ourselves permission.

The permission to stop running scared,
to stop caring about the opinions of others.

The permission to leave our comfort zone, which resembles a
pine box.

The permission to pursue the career of our dreams
and the soul mate who unflinchingly loves and supports us
every step of the way...

Permission to love,
to live,
to apologize,
and to let go.

Permission to write freely
without the pressures of delivering a bestseller.
To feel a gamut of emotions
without keeping ourselves in check.

We owe it to ourselves
to design our own destiny
and live a life we love.

I am no longer waiting on the imaginary starting line.
I am giving myself permission.
I hope you find it in your heart
to do the same.

QUIET STREET

I left work early and
rushed to the grocery store
to pick up the ingredients for your favorite meal.

I cooked dinner and
opened a bottle of your favorite wine, the 2012 Cabernet you
became obsessed with on our trip to Napa Valley a few years
ago.
I carefully set the table,
lit some candles, and waited.

Now, I'm sitting on the bench near our windowsill facing the
driveway.
The rain pelted steadily for the past few hours
and I'm already on my third bottle of wine.

My messages have gone unanswered,
and you haven't called to say that you're running late.

There are no headlights on our quiet street,
so I know you're not on your way.

Our neighbors have long retired for the evening,
and I should be asleep as well.

The clock is about to strike 2am, and I have yet to move a
muscle.

The intoxicating aroma of our dinner has long dissipated.
The candles have diminished,
and the house, like our quiet street, is covered in darkness.

2 A.M.

They tell me that
2 a.m. is a time for lovers.
For artists,
for creatives,
and for those who can't sleep because they are obsessed with
perfecting their craft.

They didn't tell me that 2 a.m. was also for the worriers.
The anxious,
the untrustworthy.

They didn't tell me that when you roll over at 2 a.m. to find
your man not in bed that your mind starts to wonder. .
Because he wasn't scheduled to go out with his boys that night,
and he was not supposed to be working late.

2 a.m. is the time for cold, hard truths.
For you to realize that your man hasn't touched you in weeks,
hasn't given you a genuine smile in what feels like an eternity.

2 a.m. reminds you that he's hardly ever home for dinner.
That he no longer sends you text messages in the middle of the
day to check on you.
That he's always "working late"
and that his friends act a little skittish around you now.
It reminds you that you don't remember the last time you two
went on a date.

15

2 a.m. reminds you of what you had,
of what you'll never recover,
and what you're still foolishly hoping can be repaired.

2 a.m. reminds you that there's only one person left in this
relationship,
and it's the fool that's lying in bed alone now.

FUCK YOU

Fuck you
And this high horse you rode in on.

You knew what you were getting into before we made this
official.
You knew the type of woman I was before you fell in love with
me.

I am not one to turn a blind eye to your indiscretions
to smile in your face when I know you're doing me dirty.

I am not docile
Or meek
Or so eager for a man that I am willing to catch whatever bones
you throw my way.

Fuck you
For being upset that I left
That I wouldn't forgive you after you disrespected me
And the sanctity of this relationship.

Fuck you
for thinking that diamonds would fix this.
Forget you for thinking an 'I'm sorry' would make it all better,

that good sex would make me forget that you broke every promise you made to me, destroying all the trust I had for you in the process.

Fuck you
For taking me for granted
And thinking that I'd always be there.

Fuck you
For letting the best thing you've ever had
Disappear from your life.

THE DANCE

I hate you for repeatedly doing this to me.
I hate you for leading me on,
For encouraging me
For sweet-talking me into thinking that we can do this again.

I thought I was the one who was unpredictable.
We both had that all wrong,
It was really you.

You weave a spell over me with your honey-drenched kisses
and hugs that reek of molasses.
With your sugar-coated words of how much you still love me
Of how you still think this can work despite the many years
we've been apart.

You tell me tales of how you would do whatever it takes to
make this work again.
Do whatever I deem necessary.
Cross-country flights to see me
Dates that begin with wine and end with us falling asleep on
my couch after a three-hour conversation.

And when I finally start to believe you,
You go ghost.
You retreat,
And we don't speak to each other again until I fit your agenda
and we start the dance all over again.

IS THIS WHAT WE'RE DOING NOW?

So, is this what we're doing now?
Lying awake
Eyes open
Backs to each other
In bed
Not touching.
Not saying a word?

Is this what we're doing now?
Passing each other in the morning, with just a head nod.
Making enough coffee for both of us and leaving a mug on the
table as a peace offering?
Walking out of the door for work without a paltry kiss or
goodbye greeting?

Is this what we're doing now?
Going to events hand-in-hand
Smiling for the cameras
Making meaningless conversation with friends
Avoiding contact but remaining enough close to maintain a
public facade?
Dropping the smile and the hand connection as soon as we get
in the car at the end of the night?

Is this what we're doing now?
Acting like strangers

Declaring war on each other?
Inflicting the silent treatment

Not kissing
Not talking
Not touching
Not making love
Not screaming
Not fighting
Not feeling?

Is this what we're doing now?
If so,
I want out.

I DESERVE

I know what I deserve
And it's not someone who makes the same promises to me
and three other women.

I know what I deserve
And it's not the months of lingering lies and mistrust.

It's not the cheap whiskey you drink after a rough day.
But the gold edition bourbon you keep in the back of the cellar
for celebratory nights.

It's not the off-the-rack designer,
But the dress with the 'by request' price sticker.

It's not the half-assed apologies you give when you know
you've messed up.
But the love that doesn't require an apology.
It's the drive that mirrors my own.
The gait that matches my determined strut along the cracked
sidewalk.

It's the love that doesn't hurt,
that doesn't question.
That doesn't have my friends messaging me with stories
they've heard of your indiscretions.

That doesn't consist of you going out to dark-lit clubs so no one will recognize you and text your picture to me.

It's the love that doesn't cause me to stay up at 2 a.m. Vacillating between questioning if it was my fault and resisting the urge to burn all of your shit.

I know what I deserve,
And it isn't you.

FREE

I reach out in the darkness
When I no longer feel your warmth.

I push my hands under the covers when the chill
starts to permeate my psyche.

I shake the sleep away when my search comes up empty.

I start to panic, just a little, when I can't find the thing I need
most to comfort me.
The thing needed to wash over me and make all right again.

But as my search intensifies,
I realize there is nothing.

No one.

And there hasn't been anyone for a while

I realized that even though the days have flown by
My heart hasn't caught up with the fact
that you are no longer available.

And as I force my heart and mind to adjust to the darkness of
the night
I know I must come to terms with the reality that I need you,
that I've always needed you.

While all you've ever needed was to be free.

OVERSTAYING MY WELCOME

The weekends are never long enough.
The evenings always too short.

The wait, always too long.
The reunion always too short.

The happiness appears fleeting,
The misery weighing me down.

The elephant on my chest hasn't moved and the desperation
for change still present.

The change is near and necessary
But I can't seem to hold on to it
To find a way to move forward.

The smile is slipping while the frown threatens to be
permanently etched.

The love is lost and now the hate is brewing.

I now turn a blind eye to the encouragements and a cheek to
the demands.

The learning curve is over and there's nothing else to do.

The teacher is gone and the class has ended.

The mentor is just a disguise for the real person lingering
beneath.

Loyalty and gratitude can no longer go hand-in-hand.

I am forever thankful but there's nothing left for me here.

And though I hope, I know it won't end well.

Because you'll think it's betrayal

It's not.

I'm human.

I need change.

I need better.

You'll think I did something wrong.

I have done many things wrong in the past
And I've owned up to those mistakes,
But I don't think you have ever acknowledged your flaws.
Your unwillingness to change,
or compromise.
Your stubbornness when it's time to admit that you're wrong.

And because of your position
You may feel as if you never have to.

I can no longer keep everything afloat
It's draining too much of my energy

And though there are still good times,
We must part while it's still okay to do so.

SO THIS IS HEARTBREAK

So this is heartbreak?
Two empty bottles of wine,
Xanax,
and popcorn strewn across my living room floor.

So this is heartbreak?
Resisting the urge to confirm if you've moved on
Or miss me
Or feel half of what I feel.

So this is heartbreak?
Waiting for my phone to ring and your face to pop up on my
screen
For you to say maybe you were wrong and that we can make
this work.
Hoping against all hope that you'll just say you're sorry.

So this is how heartbreak feels?

Waiting for you
Watching for you

Longing for you
with a pain that makes my teeth ache
and my head spin,
with a vice around my heart that threatens to tighten with each
breath.

Is this what heartbreak feels like?
Thinking I had it all but now knowing it was all a lie?

TIMESTAMPS

I was searching through old bins and came across a box filled
with items I thought I'd long discarded.
It was buried so deeply beneath papers and little knick knacks
that
I don't think I was ever supposed to find it.

Pictures of us together.
Me smiling,
Your eyes never leaving my face.
On excursions,
at your parents house,
at restaurants you dragged me to,
insisting I leave my comfort zone.

There was a picture for every occasion.

You believed in that.
Making memories,
creating timestamps.

The first necklace you bought me, the one you had engraved
with my initials, is
tucked away in the same box you gifted me with.
I remember the day you gave it to me.
I was preparing to leave and you burst through the door with
the biggest grin on your face and your hands behind your back.

Elated because you knew how much I wanted that damn
necklace.

I wore that thing every day,
Between my breasts, close to my heart.
And when we broke up, I tucked it away because it became a
constant reminder of what I could never have again, you.

There are letters I wrote to you that I never let you read.
The pages now yellowed and moth-bitten because of how long
they've been in this box,
with no air,
no light.

I start to open them up and read but I don't have to.
Like a wave, it all comes rushing back to me.

I know what I said, what was on my heart,
and I can't afford to rehash old wounds.

This box needs to be tossed.
Too many timestamps of a period that should never be
revisited.
Of a distant life.
Of a love that almost buried me.

It isn't a highlight reel,
It's spoiled footage,
of things that need to be left on the cutting room floor.

LOSS FOR WORDS

I sat down and tried to paint a picture of you
but I couldn't find the right colors
to perfectly match your hue.
To properly blend
to create the shades that
convey your complexity.

I pulled out my notebook to write you a letter and I stopped
after the first sentence.
The emotions were coursing through my veins as the pen
shook in my hand, but nothing found its way to the paper.
I knew what I wanted to tell you, what I needed to tell you,
what I had to tell you.
But they were enveloped in feelings of regret,
love to which I am no longer the recipient,
nervousness because I don't know how you'd react,
and anger because I helped to create this situation.

I tried and failed.
I tried again, and I failed once more.
So for the first time in my life,
I was at a loss for words.

ANYTIME. ANYWHERE. ANYPLACE.

I heard about your dad, and my heart briefly stopped.

I wanted to drive the six hours to see you, to hold you in my arms, and rock you while you grieve. I knew that you'd be strong for your mother and your sister but as soon as you closed the door to your apartment that you would break down. I didn't want you to endure that alone.

I pray to God you weren't alone.

I know how much he meant you.
How he was your hero,
the moral compass by which you lived.

I remember the stories you told me, of him helping you with your math homework, taking days off to drive you to those all-day science fairs.

You told me of the time you wrecked his vintage Chevy three days after you got your license. He didn't yell or ground you; he merely ruffled your hair, told you mistakes happened, and made you work six months straight with him after school to pay for the damages.

I remember you saying how much you loved him.
I remember seeing the adoration on your face and hearing it in your tone when you spoke of him.

I recall how sweet your dad was to me.
He was always quick with a smile, the first one to leave the
porch when he saw me with bags, leading up to your childhood
home. He came to most of my events, front row, cheering me
on. He read all of my blog posts and would send me notes on
the ones he really liked.

He pushed me to write more, to love more, to open up more.

I still called him every other Sunday.
I don't know if he told you that.
We laughed.
We talked about you a lot, but we mainly talked about him and
his life growing up; about the success he was able to attain, the
things he was able to acquire.
He told me how hard it was in the beginning, working long
hours, not seeing his family, only to not see immediate results
of his efforts.
He told me how he almost lost your mother, and after a year of
separation, he was able to win her back and that the
manifestation of that renewed love was you.
He told me he'd go through all of that heartache again if it
meant that he would get his wonderful son.

He sent me flowers every birthday,
Gave me a call every Christmas.
I'll miss him.

But not nearly as much as you will.

He was your best friend,
your biggest supporter,
and the confidante you needed in your times of struggle.

I want to wrap you in my love,
to give you my strength.
I want to share the burden with you
until you feel that you're okay to handle it on your own.
But I don't know if I can do that since it's been so long.
So I'll send you a message and hope that my words convey
everything I feel at this time.
And to remind you of the promise we made to each other years
back:
that I'm here if you ever need me.

At anytime, anywhere, for anything.

TUG OF WAR

You push, I pull away.
You walk toward me and I run.

You smile and I wonder if it's genuine.

You are willing to give me everything; I am prepared to give you nothing.

You tell me you love me and I can't quite seem to find my voice.
I try to return the sentiment but I can't form the words.
No sound comes when I open my mouth.

This is a game of tug of war.

A slightly dangerous game as there is so much on the line, for both of us.

One of us has to fall
And knowing the damage I can do,
I pray it isn't you.

NOT TOO CLOSE

Don't come too close.
It's not that I'll recoil; it's that once I let you pass this barrier
and into this space,
you may never want to leave.

Once I let you in, I may forbid you to leave my sight.

Don't come too close.
You won't burn but you'll feel the fire.
You may feel the suffocation and anxiety,
and all this emotion may be too much, too soon, and you may
want to run.

I won't let you, though.

Once you give me your heart, it's mine forever.
Once you give me a piece of your soul, I'll always safeguard it.
Once you give me a book, I'll write you a love letter for every
day we're together.

I'll turn you hot and then cold.
I'll make you love and hate me at the same time.

I'll feed your soul and fuel your fire,
spark your creativity and push you close to the edge.

Be very careful,
because I'll either be the best thing that's ever happened to you
or the one thing that finally breaks you.

THE REAL ME

You don't love me.
You love the illusion of me.
The mystique,
the face that I show to the world.

You love the smile that is always on my face,
the loud laugh that projects a few feet away.

You love my intellect,
quick wit,
and lovable aura.

But you don't really love ME.
Because I've never shown you who I truly am.

You've never been around me long enough to notice the kinks
in the armor.
We've never talked long enough for you to hear the crack in my
voice.
You've never seen the scared, depressed me.
The one who is paranoid that she'll never reach the pinnacle of
success she's dreamed of.
The one who doesn't know if she'll ever have a family to call
her own.
The one who lies awake at night because the fear of never
being good enough threaten to kill her.

You don't love me,
and I understand why.
Because who can love someone they've never truly known?

DON'T BLAME ME

I told you to be careful
To watch your six,
to proceed with caution,
to have an abundance of patience.

You agreed, but I now I see you didn't heed my warning.
You thought I was bluffing.
You thought I was scared,
and you thought that you could change me.

You wanted more than I knew how to give.
You wanted all my love,
at a time when it wasn't mine to give.

Don't blame me because you're hurt now.
This could have been avoided.
You didn't listen,
and you moved before it was time.

Don't blame me
because I told you what could happen.
you chose to enter the ring anyway
and you lost.

Don't blame me,
I didn't mean to hurt you.
I was only trying to warn you.

RESTLESS

Restless nights
Tossing and turning
TV on mute because complete darkness now haunts me.

Night fits
Kicking off the covers
Groaning with frustration
Mind racing with endless thoughts

Worrisome sleep
Dreamless nights
or worst,
dreams filled with terror

Agonizing if I'll ever make it.
If my dreams are too unattainable,
Goals too lofty.

If my work ethic will ever be enough
If I'll ever get to live the audacious life I vividly envision every
day.

Fluttering eyelashes
Anxious while thinking about whether I can ever balance it all
If I can have the "everything" we all talk about.
Wondering if I'll ever make my family proud
If I'll ever be proud of myself.

If the self doubt will ever cease
If the anxiety will ever lessen
If I'll ever realize that the strain I put on myself is unhealthy
If the elephant sitting on my chest will ever move.

I don't have the answers when I'm staring at the ceiling late at
night.
But let's hope I find them soon,
so that there will be fewer restless nights.

FAILURE

It's hard not to feel like a failure nowadays.
The shame threatens to smother me,
as I look out and hope for someone to show me some empathy.

It's hard not to feel like a failure,
when I turn to comparison, not as motivation,
but as a way to beat myself up because of all that I lack.

I'm the one people come to for guidance,
yet I have no guidance for myself.
No guide,
No alchemist,
only a dusty road with no signs.

It's hard not to feel like a failure,
when I've always been the one with the grandiose dreams,
yet have not done the work to realize them.
My compass is broken,
or at least it feels like it is
when I look around and see people's highlight reels
and try to stupidly compare that to the full, unedited version of
my life that only I see daily.

It's hard not to feel like a failure,
when I've yet to define success on my own terms.
If I don't know what accomplishment looks like for me,
I'll never be satisfied with what I have.

So I guess that's what I need to do.
What I've always told my friends to do.
Determine what my success looks like,
so that I'll make it hard to feel like a failure.

DROWNING

I'm drowning
and no one even notices.

I'm swerving off the road
and no one grabs the steering wheel,
to stop me from crashing.

I don't know if I can climb any higher.
No one is giving me a boost from behind,
to encourage me to keep going or to offer a cheering word.

Sometimes it gets hard to breathe
and no one offers me an oxygen mask.

My head spins and the world starts to tilt
But no one is there to steady me.

The head dips and the smile slips
and no one lifts my chin up.

Sometimes I feel alone
and there is no one to comfort me

To understand,
To bother to genuinely ask.

It hurt for a moment.
Okay, maybe even longer than that.
but it won't break me.
Not yet anyway.

Because as long as the ink continues to drip out of this pen,
The words will jump onto the paper.

These journals will prove to be cathartic.

As the words continue to flow smoothly beneath this fine point
pen
And onto the aged parchment paper,
I'll find the oxygen.
I'll see the finish line.
I'll notice the break and
the sun beaming through the water.

I'll swim to shore and
I'll feel the sun against my face
when I first emerge from the crystalline water.

I'll taste the salt on my tongue
and I'll feel the knots in my hair.

And I'll know that I made it out.

DO YOU KNOW I'M ALIVE?

Can you hear how loud and fast my heart is beating?
Can you realize how claustrophobic it now feels?
It's because my anxiety consumes every nook and cranny.
Did you sense how quickly I took all the air out of the room
when I walked in?
Can you feel my anguish?
Is my cry loud enough?
Or does the momentary silence pierce through your skull?

I've been barely present,
hardly speaking
not even writing.
I'm here but I don't know if you've seen me.

Do you even know if I'm alive?
Well, do you?

I PROMISE

Is it okay if I cry just this one time?
Just one time, I promise.
No one will see me: I'll make sure of it.

Is it okay if I scream just this one time?
Just once.
No one will hear me. I promise.

Is it okay if I stop pretending to be strong for just five minutes?
No one will know the truth. I promise.
No one will know that I don't constantly smile.
That sometimes I'm not as strong as I pretend to be.

No one will know that I have demons.
Fears.
Secrets.
Things that keep me awake at night.

Can I just have these five minutes to cry?
To scream,
To lose myself.
I'll put myself back together. I promise.

WHAT IS IT ABOUT US?

What is about me that turns you hot and cold?
That makes you leave but then run back years later?

What is about me that pushes you away but then internally
begs you to stay?
What is about me that makes you want to kiss me one minute
and strangle me the next?

What is about you that makes me daydream while I'm at work?
That keeps your image at the forefront of my mind?
that makes my back arch,
my lips spread,
my heart race and
my mind wander?

What is that makes me play back every single moment
we've ever spent together in excruciatingly vivid detail.

What is about us that leaves us screaming one minute and
breathless with wonder the next?

What is about us that we just can't seem to shake?

LOOKING FOR YOU

I look for you in every man I've dated since...
I look to see if they wear a suit the way you do, if their smile
illuminates every corner of the room like yours does.

Do they know how to ply me with words that make me feel like
I've won an argument, only to realize I've done everything they
wanted me to do?

Is their voice like silk? Do they have the inflections that find a
way to make me angry then make me laugh, and then calm me,
all in one conversation?

Can we stay on the phone for hours while never running out of
things to say?

Do I pine for them the way I did for you?
Does my heart race when someone mentions their name the
way it still does when I hear yours?

Does he make me think of the future?
Of a family I didn't dare to dream about? A relationship I never
thought could be mine?

I look for you in every man I thought I loved.
I stare into their eyes and wait for the truth to reveal itself.
I wait for their touch to caress me the way yours did.

I wait for them to make my day better when I send a text or
pick up the phone,
only to be sorely disappointed.

I look for the wrong things in the wrong men, and it's not their
fault.
They don't know who they're up against,
What and who I'm comparing them to.

They're in a game they don't know how to play, fighting a
battle they didn't sign up for
The odds are stacked against them, and there's no way they
can ever win, not against you.

I look for you everywhere, in everyone, yet you're nowhere to
be found.

DEAR LOVE

All I ask is that you be my peace.
My sanctuary.
My safe space.

I don't need you to be this idea of perfection that we think we
need.

I just need you to provide the balance in the craziness that is
my life.

I have God; I have friends, and I have family that I can lean on
but the partner that can bring me the peace I need is what I'm
missing.

I would rather laugh with you than lie to you.
Cry with you than cry because of you.

I would rather grow old with you than fight with you and live
my days without you.

Dear Love,
I crave you
I need you
I want you
I may not be entirely ready, but will I ever?
Can we try?
Can we see what happens if an opportunity presents itself?

I won't force it; it's going to have to happen naturally.
I just hope I haven't let it pass me by.
I hope I haven't blocked my blessings.

Dear Love,
I know you want me as much as I want you.
Please don't go.

4-PAGE LETTER

I want to write you a letter
that carries the scent of my perfume
so that when you open the envelope
and read my words,
all you'll do is think of me.

In my letter,
I'll tell you all of my truths,
share of all my dreams,
finally be real with you about where I see us
and who I want us to be.

I don't want to do this dance
where we try to dissect what this is.

I want to enjoy it,
go on dates,
meet your mother
and discover your plans for the future.

I don't care how many degrees you have or
what school you went to.

I want to know if your heart is pure

If you have ambition,
if you want more out of life.

I want to go on trips where
we find out if we can tolerate each other in the
exclusivity of our own presence.

I want to go to the south of France,
to Greece,
or maybe backpack through Europe.

I want a romantic getaway somewhere in the Caribbean
or even to the wineries in Napa Valley.

I want you to stay close,
to my body,
to my heart,
to my soul,
and in the deep recesses of my mind.

I'm writing you this letter
so that I can finally be honest with you,
and hope that you can do the same.

I want you to write me a letter
that carries the scent of your cologne
so that when I open the envelope
and read your words,
All I'll do is think of you.

THE POWER OF THE WRITTEN WORD

"I love you."

Shouldn't that be enough?
Shouldn't that help to wash away the fear?

Shouldn't that be enough?
To get us through,
to see past all the fog?

"You're everything to me."

Shouldn't that be confirmation?
That I'm here
and I'm not going anywhere
despite your attempts at sabotage?
Despite your antics and
sometimes unforgivable nature?

"I'm here to stay."

Shouldn't that prove loyalty?
Commitment?

Or is it that words don't mean much to you anymore?

If that's the case, then we're at a crossroads
because words mean everything to me.

Always have,
always will.
I thought you understood that.

Understood my need for putting words to paper,
for whispering them in your ear when no one is around,
for leaving notes strategically placed for you to find.

It's what I do best.
It's how I communicate.
It's what I prefer and what has always worked well for me.

Actions speak louder than words, they say
but I don't know if that's ever been my reality.

I can tell you better than I can show you, at times.

That's the gift and the curse.

Words are permanent and you can't take them back.
They are forever etched in your memory,
and very often, your heart.

They consume you,
like the bone chill of winter
even when you make a roaring fire
and cover yourself in the warmest of blankets

Like when the wind travels with you
as you cruise down the open road

with the top down.
Like the lingering forehead kiss you give before you leave.

Like the faint scent of your cologne when you leave the room.

Words last forever and that's why I use them.

I may not always know how to act,
How to provide the right touch,
How to do the right things in public when we're together,
but I'll never lack for words.

To say how I feel,
to tell you what you mean to me.

To say that your intellect is an aphrodisiac
and that I find you so fine that most days, I can't wait to get
you alone.

I'll never lack for words
to say that your touch always causes a shiver to trickle down
my spine,
that your promises give me hope,
that the love that's always in your eyes makes my day,
that the way you encourage me makes me proud,
that the warmth of your body next time mine melts away the
stress of from a bad day.

I have no problem saying these things -
writing these letters

You can't change me
But we can compromise.
And my hope is that you hold my words in high regard
and let it wrap you up in a cocoon that always makes you feel
protected.

UNBREAKABLE

This is my toast
to all the lessons we continue to learn
to the stories we'll never tell
to the ones we will that will make every bestseller list.

This is a toast to us,
to our love,
to our lives,
to every decision we've ever made - for better or for worse.

Here's a toast to us our bond,
The one that we've long deemed unbreakable.

STRIPPED BARE

Love has stripped me bare.
You have stripped me bare.
All of the extra layers have been peeled back.
All of the walls have come crashing down,
and it isn't even something that was planned.

The mask is off.
It just happened.
Shit, you just happened.

You opened my eyes, my heart, and allowed me to see the
beauty of this thing that we call love - especially when it is
done right.

The mask is off.
The one I wear for the public, the face I put on for everyone to
see.

You've managed to look past all of that - and strip the layers I
use to protect myself from the bullshit.
You've done it so expertly that it scares me.

You know the real me, the one who is afraid to show all of
herself in fear of rejection.

You saw me and didn't run.

You've allowed me to grow into the person that I'm still hoping to become.

You've shown me that it's okay to remove the mask, to let some people see the real me
because it is only then that I can let in the light.

THE CALM IN THE MIDDLE OF THE STORM

You're the first thing on my mind when I wake up,
and the last thing before I go to sleep.

I close my eyes and for a moment
I can feel you near me.
Your head nestled in the crook of my neck and collarbone
as you've told me that's your favorite way to fall asleep.
Right before you settle in, you kiss me behind my ear
and whisper small snatches of loving words to me
whenever the mood strikes you.

And in that moment,
I feel wanted.
Beautiful.

But then again, I always feel that way with you.

Whether it's late at night when my hair's already tied up
and I'm curled up on the sofa watching my favorite show.
You pat me on my thigh,
give me a brief kiss and leave me be,
You don't interrupt my time but patiently wait until I am done
when you know that you will have my undivided attention.
You're always present, even when you give me space.

It still amazes me how you never go too long without touching
me

Your fingers in my hair
A pull on my shirt
A nudge on the cheek with your nose
A grab of my hand
or a stolen kiss in the unlikeliest of places.

It amazes me that you do all of this, and I let you.

Sometimes, I think you may know me better than I know
myself
and I'm not always happy about that.
You instantly know when I've had a bad day
when to retreat and when to force me closer.

This isn't picture perfect but I'll take it over everything else.

I aggravate the hell out of you.
When I need attention, I can get annoyingly clingy.

I don't like to comb my hair
and I choose to go without makeup
at the most inopportune times.

I don't cook and I'm nowhere near a size four.
I'm not used to a genuine partnership so
my first instinct is generally to shut down when we have an
argument.

There are very few things that I can give you that
you cannot provide for yourself,

and that haunts me the most.

But my heart is pure.
The love is real.
The growth is there.

I may not be the perfect partner but I'll be more than enough
for you.

No one will hold you down like I do.
Take care of you like I can,
pray for you like I will.

You lift me up, encourage me,
and constantly provide support, so for that,
there's very little that I won't do for you.

You think you've had love before
but not until you've met me.

There have been others before me
but I can guarantee there'll never be
one quite like me after.

I've ruined you for everyone else.

This love we share is all encompassing.

It's terrifying yet beautiful.
It can be chaotic at times

but it will always be our calm during a storm.

TOUCH. TASTE. SMELL.

My name rolls off your tongue like syrup from the bottle
as you pour it onto my favorite chocolate chip pancakes.
Your tone is forever sweet like the powdered sugar
you sprinkle over Belgian waffles.
Your hugs are like coffee, first thing in the morning,
warm, strong, and complete with a lingering aroma that
sometimes causes my eyes to close in reminiscence.

Your kisses are like my grandmother's cookies.
I always snuck the first one when no one was looking, but then
remembered how addictive they were and shamelessly got my
fill.

Your love is like my mama's okra soup,
nourishing me, leaving no room for extras,
leaving absolutely no room for doubt.

COMFORT FOOD

You're like my favorite comfort foods.
Bad for me in the best possible way.

After a rough day, I walk into the house and throw my things
on the floor and grab a pint of ice cream as I strip on my way to
the couch.
With the shades still closed, and the quiet filling the
apartment, I open what should be a banned substance with
one hand and call you with the other.

I wait for your voice to break the line.

You always know why I'm calling based on the time of the day.
You sense my quiet over the phone and know that I don't really
want to rehash anything at the moment. So, you go into a spiel
about your day, your upcoming projects, your brother who
constantly annoys you, and the cousin you had to bail out of
trouble yet again.

You're like a savory home-cooked Sunday meal with all the
trimmings. The food that sticks to your sides, and though you
don't feel the repercussions right away, continuous
indulgences have you letting out your dresses and sizing up
your jeans.

You're like the last piece of chocolate that I know I should l leave for someone else to have, but I simply can't resist. . I always know that I'm going to regret it later but in the moment, I don't care about that.

The first taste is pure decadence; the remaining bites are always scrumptious. I never regret it at the time, but give me a few hours or days, and I'm beating myself up over repeating destructive behaviors.

You're always good to me in the moment.
Like I'm sure you're good to everyone else in their moments.
You're the extra chocolate chips I toss liberally into my batter when I bake. An amazing addition but one that needs to be added sparingly.
Other people love the same comfort food, which is why I try not to get too attached.

It's for everybody, and you've proven that you're for everybody.

It pisses me off but I can't stay angry for long because I know what purpose you serve in my life.

I don't need you. I can probably live without you; at least that's what I tell myself.
But here's the thing about comfort food: while I want to stop eating it, I can't.

It's called "comfort food" for a reason.

I don't need it all the time but I have to allow myself the comfort when I do.

Every time I get a taste, it's heavenly and it's the temporary balm to the ailment that's been paining me.

MORE

I'm going to need a little more.

I get that you're content with your current efforts.
The women in your past have been okay with letting you
scrape by,
with just giving the bare minimum.

You're a man of substance,
a man who's successful in just about every way
and most women would die for you to look at them with just a
smidgen of interest.
So when you do, they take whatever you can give them.
whatever you're willing to give them,
the small morsels of love,
the intermittent bouts of affection.

They've been okay with you not giving your whole heart,
with you telling them some spiel about how you've been hurt
before so you tread lightly.
Part of that may be true, but that weak excuse won't fly with
me,
And you know it.

We're doing things a little differently now.
The game plan is going to have to change.

I'm going to need all of you.

I'm going to need you to feed my soul.
To be my muse,
To help me paint my masterpiece.

I'm going to need more,
and I won't stop until I have it all.

THIS ISN'T THE FAIRYTALE THEY TOLD ME ABOUT

Not every situation is a fairytale.
Not everyone gets their happy ending.
But that doesn't make it any less a love story.

Is it perfect? Hell no.
Is it worth it? Well, that depends on whom you ask.

It's unforgiving
Uncompromising
Unrelenting
Painful
Devastating

But for all its unsavory elements, it is extraordinary.

It is that "once in a lifetime" type of love.
It is the "I didn't know I could really feel this way about
someone" type of love

It is the "I've wanted this feeling but didn't dare dream it could
be mine" type of love.
It is the "I will do whatever I can to make you happy" type of
love.

It is the "I will love you until my very last breath" type of love.
Regardless of the flaws,
the imperfections,

the power struggles and the constant back and forth.
This isn't the shit you read about in books or see played out on screen.
This can be dangerous if we're unable to control it.
Destructive yet mesmerizing.

But we have to see how this will play out.
We have to weigh the pros and cons.

The reality of this situation, for people in our predicament, is that we have to work twice as hard.
We have to keep a tighter rein our control.
Because we can be unpredictable.

Given the chance, one of us will revert to our old ways.
Become self destructive, push the other one away because it's too much.
And we'll feel undeserving, unworthy.
Sooner or later, that gets old.
And the other stops fighting because as much as we want them to, we can't rely on anyone to "fix" us.

We have to fix ourselves.
Become whole on our own.

They can help us along the way, but they can't start the process for us.

So if we do succeed and push them away, yes, they'll be gone
from our life, from our immediate grasp, but they'll never be
gone from our heart.
Because this kind of love is tricky.
This truly can be that one person who 'gets' you.
This could be that one person who carves out such a huge place
in your heart that you wouldn't know how to function if they
don't remain in that place.

It doesn't mean that you can't love anyone else but it does
mean that you will never probably feel that way about someone
again.

It means that regardless of future loves,
If the other needs you, you will drop everything and go to
them.
Anytime, any place, for anything.
To help them.
To be there for them.
To remind them why they are here.
Because no matter what, you're drawn to each other.
By life,
by love,
by whatever fucked-up situation life has thrown at you.

It's messy,
It's complicated,
And at times, it's confusing as hell.

It's not a fairytale,
but it's my truth.
It's yours
It's ours.

We claim it.
We embrace it,
and despite it all, we are thankful for it.
And we don't apologize for it.

MEDIOCRITY

We settle for too many things in life.
Love should not be one of them.

I want the feeling of love to threaten to overwhelm me.
I want to wrap myself in it.

I want to drown in you
In your gaze.
Your touch,
in the sound of your voice.

I want spontaneity.

I want sex on the beach with the moonlight as our only guide.

I want love in the park under the swings.

I want a quick fuck in the car on the way to the club.

I want a dance at night in our room by the bed
because we turned on the radio and our
favorite record is playing.

I want you to tell me your greatest dreams.
I want you to trust me to believe in them as much as you do.
Because I will push you to your destiny
as you encourage me to aim higher.

I want you to tell me about your nightmares as I quietly
whisper my fears.

I don't want mediocrity when it comes to love.
I want heart-racing, blood-pumping, overwhelmingly beautiful
Breathtaking
"You will never forget me" love.

Where you'll be everything I've ever wanted
and I'll be all the things you never thought to dream of.

That's what I want,
I know you want that too.

MISCONCEPTIONS

The misconception is that I need you to be perfect.
That I need us to be perfect.
That I need everything to work flawlessly and
that is simply not true.
I still believe that fairy tales exist,
and that we all have at least one soulmate, but I am not naive.

I know that battles are not won without sacrifice, without a
little pain.

I know we must have endurance and that we will have to fight
to persevere.
I don't need you to be rich - to lavish me with expensive
trinkets and material gestures of affection.
What I really need from you is your patience and
your understanding because I'm sure I'll need it. I need to
know that you're willing to share my burdens.
I'm often afraid.
I'll try to run.
I need to know that you're willing to climb into bed with me,
and hold me
securely until the clouds clear and the storm passes.

I don't need you to fix me - I know that I have to do that on my
own.

I do need you to share the pain every now and then, though.

To be the balm that soothes the ache.
To help me chase away the fear when it threatens to stifle me.

I need to know that I can share my dreams with you
my every wish, my every goal.
I need to know that you'll always be in my corner,
helping me do whatever it takes to achieve the success I so
desperately crave.

I don't need you to be anyone other than yourself.
I don't need you to do any more than your personal best.

What I do need is for you to just be here, in this moment, with
me

Until death.
After life.

To show me that this is real - to help me navigate the waters in
this thing we call life.

To constantly remind me of what extraordinary feels like.

THE WAITING GAME

I know it's too bold of me to ask, but I'm putting it out there
anyway.
I know I have no right but I have to.

Can you just wait?
Please?
I'm not ready to say goodbye.
I'm not ready for you to walk out of my life.
It was temporary before, but I know this time, it'll be
permanent and it'll be my fault.
You're always putting forth the effort, and I'm always blocking
it.
I'm the practical one that blocks you at every turn.
Telling you why it can't work.
Why we aren't meant to be.

I don't even believe that.
But I'm afraid.
And I don't want to disappoint you.
I don't want you to change your mind.
So a part of me thinks I should sabotage it
before you do.

Protect myself before you break me.
Before I break us.

I know it's wrong.

And I'm trying.
So, I need you to wait.

Just wait.
I still need more time
to discover your dreams, for you to hear about mine.
For you to whisper my name as only you can.

Just, wait.
Please.

I'm not ready
to never hear your voice again,
to never rub my fingers down your spine.
to never hear your laugh,
or see your smile.

Just wait.
I know I always promise to be better,
to do better,
to say more of what I mean.
And I almost always renege on that promise.
But this time, it's different - I swear.

Wait.
Wait for me.
Wait on me.
I'm not ready yet, and deep down, I know you're not either.
Whether it's 10 days or 10 years, don't close the door on us.

Don't you dare say goodbye.

You're not ready.
I'm not ready
to face the truth
and accept that the past is what's keeping us together and that
we're only good in theory yet not in practice.

I'm not ready for you to never say "I love you" again.

We're both still waiting
on when it feels right to say goodbye

So until we both feel that, let's just wait.

I DIDN'T BELIEVE

I didn't believe you
or what you said to me.

I questioned your intentions,
your motivation.

I didn't believe you,
in what you promised.

I didn't believe you were sincere,
that your motives were pure.

I didn't know how to accept your white hot truth.
Your patience,
your fire,
your light that burned brightly,
not dimming mine but only making it brighter.

I didn't believe you
or what you had to offer me.

I claimed I wanted it all, but I had no clue how to handle it.
How to accept it.

I told you I would give you everything, but I lied.
I gave you nothing because I didn't believe you.

I didn't believe that you would help me.
Protect me
Please me
Love me
Understand me.

I didn't believe you
or your efforts.

I didn't acknowledge your hard work,
or the countless times you gave me another chance.

I thought you would be an anchor
that would keep me in one place when all I wanted to do was
move.

I couldn't let that happen,
so I chose not to believe you
or the voice in the my head that said
I should give you a chance.
that I should let you in,
love you like I know I could.

I didn't believe you,
so I pushed you away.

I let you sit
and rot
and resent

until you had no other choice but to walk away

I didn't believe you
and now you're gone
and there's no one to blame
but myself.

SCREW UP

I think I fucked up.
Years ago, we had the makings of something beautiful
but too much was in the way.

There was constant chatter.
Insecurity.
Naiveté
and I was scared, and I did what I do best: I ran.

I didn't let it run its course.
I ended it early, stopped the bus before it reached its
destination.
I got off and I didn't look back.

Or maybe I did?

Because now, many years have passed, and there are lingering
questions and a tinge of regret.

I'm not sure if I was right.
If I did the right thing.
If I should have given it more time.

I hear about your accomplishments, and what your life is like
now,
and it appears that you're moving on.
and for a minute, I stop.

I'm a little taken aback
Because sometimes when I hear those things, I feel like I'm
stuck and you're not.

I start to reminisce.

About what was.
What wasn't.
And what could have been.

I was young, inexperienced, insecure, and shallow.

I let the doubt rear its ugly head.
I let the worry cloud my judgment
and I let the uncertainty seep through my pores.

I should have held on,
and not hold back.

I could have held on
and given you a glimpse of the real me.

But I didn't
and I let it go.
I let you go
and at the time; I thought it was best.

Now?
I'm not sure.

Deep down, these feelings of regret may not truly be real.

Deep down, I feel like it could have never worked out in the long run.

I guess I'm just selfish and wanted a bit more time.

I wasn't ready
and I think you also knew that.
Which is why you didn't overly question my decision.
I've always wanted what was best for you,
you know that.
And I refuse to stifle your growth because of what I am
incapable of giving.

I thought you were more than I could handle.
Or maybe it just wasn't enough.

The fire that I am constantly chasing wasn't there,
And I didn't want to start to miss it.

I knew all of that then,
I know all of this now.
But it doesn't stop my mind from wondering,
From being curious
From thinking 'What if?

SELFISH

I'm selfish - you know this; I do too.

You appear seemingly happy, and I'm not, so I get angry for a
split second,
thinking about what I let get away.
The things I did.
The words I said.

And I wonder whether I can get you to look at me like you used
to, just one more time?

But that's wishful thinking, isn't it?

We're two completely different people now, on separate paths,
and we are better for it.
There was never a real chance that we would make it.
There were far too many obstacles.

Doesn't mean I miss you any less, though.

Doesn't mean that on certain nights,
when the merlot is flowing and the candles are dim
that I don't wait for you,
watch for you
imagine you with me.

I just need to see you,
one more time.
For the first time
in countless years.

I need to trace your jawline
and commit your face to memory.

I need to hold onto you
for a second too long when you hug me, so I can inhale your
scent
and carry it with me.

I need to look into your eyes.
Those eyes that always comforted me,
to see that smile one more time.
The twinkle when I ask if you're doing alright.

I need you to squeeze my hand for just a second too long
when no one is watching.

I just need to see you again,
one more time.

To see if **it** is still there
if it even was there at all
or if it all was just a figment of my imagination.

I just need to see you again,
one more time,
to make sure you weren't the one who got away.

I'M SORRY

I'm sorry
I couldn't be what you wanted.
What you needed.
What you so desperately craved.

It's not that I didn't want to,

It's not that I didn't think we could be beautiful,
because I knew we would be.

It's not that I didn't trust it or you.
It's that I didn't trust myself.

I'm sorry I couldn't live up to expectations.
I'm sorry I couldn't abide by the promises I so desperately
wanted to keep.

I'm sorry I couldn't love you the way you deserve
In the way I tried to love you.

I loved you before I knew what love was.
Before I knew how to breathe life into myself, much less
another human being.

I'm sorry it took so long to apologize.
To admit my faults
to know I fucked up.

I had to figure it out,
and by the time I did,
it was already too late.

IT WAS ALL A DREAM

I used to dream about this, you know.
About you,
about me,
about us,
about your raspy voice when you call me at the crack of dawn
because you want to be the first thing I hear when I wake up.

About your lazy smile being the first thing I see when I open
my eyes in the morning.
With your head propped up on one hand, you use the other to
trail a path down my body as you wait for me to rise so you
can kiss me before you get up for work.
And then tease me about my morning breath and the heavy
snores that kept you awake the night before.

I used to dream about a family.
Our family.
In the dream, we'd have a few children;
boys who would be your little clones
with their rugged demeanor and personable attitude.
Girls, with your kind eyes and my loud mouth , who would
wrap you around their finger.
I dreamt about trips to Australia and Paris and our beautiful
cabin in the mountains
where the snow falls continuously,
and I watch it for hours from the window nook
as I plot out details of my next book.

I dreamt of making love on our deck as the sun sets.
Rendezvous in the backseat of the two-door Camaro you
insisted on buying.
Quickies in the office before your next meeting.

You cooking me dinner.
Me giving you massages.
You saying "I love you"
Me making you promise to never let me go.

But I don't have that dream anymore, do I?
Because you were right, like you often times are.

I was too afraid to truly believe, to take that leap, so the
dreams are just that.
All that's left is the cold dose of reality of what could have
been.

COME BACK TO ME

I love you

Knowing me the way you do, you know those three words don't
come easily for me.
You know it's not something that I take lightly.
You know it's not something I've said to any other man but
you.

I love you.
Not because I should
or because everyone says we would be good together.
I love you because I don't know how not to.
I love you without rationalization.
Without reservation.
Without hesitation.

You've seen me at my worst and loved me anyway.
You've loved me before I truly knew what love meant.
Brought me joy when all I felt was pain.
Shown me light when all I could see was the darkness.
Given me strength when I was too weak to stand on my own.

You've been the whisper of cool breeze on a hot summer day
The heat from a crackling fire on the coldest winter night.

I love you

I miss you...

I need you.

Come back to me.
Please.

MESSAGE IN A BOTTLE

Whenever the phone rings late at night, there's a part of me
that hopes it's you.
A very small piece that gets smaller everyday - but it's still
there, much to my chagrin.
I wonder if you even still have my number or if yours is still the
same?

A part of me always regretted the way things ended.
I pushed you away when all I wanted was to bring you closer.
I didn't know how to handle the intensity; I was still young and
naïve. I did the only thing I knew how to do, and in the end, I
hurt both of us.
I did that.
I know that, and now I accept that.

You seemed to recover much quicker than I did.
It was something that I expected though, to be honest.
Maybe it was because I thought you always had more invested,
or maybe it was because it meant a lot more to me than I led
on.
Maybe it meant less to you than you claimed.

Either way, it's done.
There's no going back,
even when it haunts me.
I won't reach out because I don't like to open old wounds.
I don't know how or what you're doing.

I don't see pictures and I don't ask our mutual friends about
you.
I scrubbed your presence clean from my home.
I burned every picture with you in it.

I don't hate you.
How can I when I was the one that messed things up?

I just don't need the constant reminders.
I don't need the memories of you in my space.

None of that is your fault;
you're a milestone I wish I took more time to celebrate.

I put this letter in a bottle and push it out into the water.
As it floats deeper into the ocean, I say a prayer and hold out
hope that someday, this will wash ashore and land right at
your feet.

You'll read it
and know it's from me,
even though it's not signed.

You'll read it and know that I remember,
know that I haven't forgotten,
and know that a piece of me will always cherish you.

HOME

I go home whenever I need to reset.

It's where the sun kisses my face,
and the water is so blue I can lose myself in it.

I go home when I need a certain stillness.
Where I can get away from the constant rush of the 9 to 5,
the brutal pace of what many may deem city life.

I go home when I need a simple nudge,
the light spin of a Rolodex,
the sharpening of a few tools.

It's the beauty and the curse of craving home.

Being home is always an overwhelmingly complicated feeling.
It calms me and helps to cancel out the noise.
It also fascinates me.
It reminds me of just how blessed I am.

However, it also reminds me how easy it is to lose yourself if
you're not careful,
how easy it is to get trapped in the beauty, the quiet, and
relative peace
until you find yourself worrying about nothing else.
I'll be the first to admit that when I force myself to will my
mind blank,

which I often do when home,
it's easy to get distracted and obsessive about that same quiet
that worries me.

Home always nourishes me,
and then threatens to cut off all of my oxygen,
stifling me to the point where I cannot breathe.
It holds me close and makes me empty promises while luring
me away from everything else.

Home is the ultimate comfort zone while serving as my biggest
critic.
It oftentimes wraps me up in both love and isolation in the
scariest of ways.
It's the breeze on a hot summer's day
the douse of cold water that awakens my senses.
It's the hope that blooms bright while also managing to be the
fear that chokes me.

It's not always the homecoming I once dreamed of, but it's
always what I need.
It's everything.
It's nothing.
It's the place I can never leave nor forget.

It's my sanctuary,
my muse,
my answers to the questions that I'm afraid to voice aloud,
the faucet that fills the drain.

Home isn't a place,
or a tangible thing.

Home is wherever you are.
Home is you.

As you always beautifully remind me,
no matter what happens,
whenever I need to and even when I don't,
I can always go home again.

GRATEFUL

I am thankful for it all because it's helped me grow.

The disappointment because I now know what to expect.
The happiness because it gives me hope.
The laughter because it gives me life.
The success because it lets me know the possibilities.
The loss because it gives me strength.
The pain because I now know I can survive.
And through that I have learned my purpose.

I didn't always like who I was but I love the person I am
becoming.
All of this has shaped me, molded and motivated me,
To achieve greatness and the things that for far too long I
thought were unattainable.

I am grateful for it all because now, it's allowed me to wear my
heart on my sleeve and allow you all to see.

ACKNOWLEDGMENTS

Writing has always been my escape. I've kept journals since I was old enough to remember; filling pages with poems, prayers I felt more comfortable writing than saying out loud; stories I made up with characters I'd fallen in love with and letters to people that I would never mail.

Although I'm pretty outspoken, I'm really an introvert. Writing has always been my go-to; I may not say what I feel all of the time, but you'll always find the truth buried within the pages of one of the hundreds of books I still have.

This book is the first of many. I hope as you flipped through the pages, you connected with the emotions, appreciated the sincerity and fall in love with the words.

To Cheryl, my mother, for being the best mama a girl can ask for.

To Kenyanna, for always indulging me in my journal habit, even now.

To Ella, who gave me the push I needed to publish this book when I let my insecurities get the best of me. My gratitude knows no bounds.

To my closest friends, your conversations give me a joy that fuel my spirit. Thank you for the years filled with laughter, hard truths and the occasional bottle of wine; many of these poems were completed as a result of those conversations. These are our stories.

ABOUT THE AUTHOR

Raised in the beautiful Turks and Caicos Islands, Natalya believes that the best way to enjoy a great book is with the soothing sound of the ocean.

Natalya attended The University of Tampa where she obtained a Bachelor of Arts degree in Communications. She assists clients as an Account Manager by day and is a writer by night.

A soap opera fanatic and an avid reader; she can usually be found with her nose in a book, writing reviews of her favorite romance novels on her blog, and perusing the shelves of her neighborhood bookstore.

Connect with Natalya
Website: www.natalyamuncuff.com
Blog: www.theislandreader.com

Twitter: https://twitter.com/NatalyaMuncuff
Facebook: https://fb.me/authornatalyamuncuff